Contents

My Christening Robe
James McGauran 1991

Our Lady and St. Patrick's Church, Ballymoney, where Mary was baptised and buried from.

The Earliest Years

I have been told that I was born at 1pm on the 12 July 1895, my cries drowned by the lambegs of Shanagy (Vow) Loyal Orange Lodge, as the band marched to Ballymoney on that Twelfth long ago. Since then I have seen ninety Twelfths and in ways I do not feel particularly old. My birth was in a little cotter's house at the Enagh, Ballymoney. My father was then working for James Mc Afee at Ballybrakes. Such cottages went with your work. Part of the time he worked labouring on their farm. At a later stage he worked on the roads as James Mc Afee had contracts carting stones to make and mend roads in the district about Ballymoney.

In those days there was no trained midwife. Mrs. Mc Afee, his wife came up the lane to attend my Mother. I remember her coming later when those a bit younger than me were born. Of course I don't remember that day, but I was told about it. I remember her coming when someone was sick and to care for other members of the family for many years afterwards..

Mr. and Mrs. Mc Afee were my sponsors at Baptism in the church of Our Lady and St. Patrick Ballymoney, where I was christened Mary, the first girl in the family. I wore a lovely antique christening robe with rows and rows of little tucks and a deep lace border. Hugh had already worn it before me. My mother said that the Reverend Jameson's wife had given it to her and it was already old then. I often wondered how the Reverend Jameson's wife came to part with such an heirloom.

Since then it has been worn by three further generations of the family. I've kept it safe in the years since and after I am gone, I expect that it will still be in use. The earliest Twelfths I don't remember, except my mother passing a few knots of flowers, marigolds and nasturtiums to the Orangemen as they passed the hedge. She would give them a drink of water to slake their thirst. On their journey home they had drunk better than the water my mother gave from her can near the doorway.

There were certainly no birthday cards for us then, but my mother always marked our birthdays with a cake of bread and a pot of raspberry or strawberry jam. Although she had 10 children each one of us was treated in a special and individual way. For ever after my birthday was marked. It was a hard day to forget. The drums beat out the march of the years, and I was never allowed to forget it. And I'm still not that anxious to be reminded that I'm well into old age, old, if I told the truth or acknowledged it. I don't feel any older inside today at 90 than I did at 19 or 9 for that matter. At the present minute I'm a wee bit unsure as to where to continue my tale. I suppose a good place to start would be to give you some account of my mother.

Birthplace at Enagh.
Enagh (Aonach - Irish for Fair), was referred to in the oldest history, long before Ballymoney, as the Peaceful Paradise. The peace at Enagh Cross was broken by the Viking raids.

"Flowering" at the turn of the century.
Shaw Collection

My Mother

My mother, Ellen Dunlop, was born in 1865 in Drumale, Aghadowey at what was then Moss Lane. Her father was Pat Dunlop and her mother had been Catherine Boyle. She had three sisters, Jane, Mary Ann and Lizzie and three brothers John, Jamie and Brian, spelt I think Bryan, who died young, of meningitis I remember my mother saying.

Her father was a small farmer, theirs was a very close community by the side of the Bann, where Dempseys, Boyles, McDonalds, Dicksons, Mitchells, Hegartys and Dunlops were related and connected in many ways in Drumale, Cornamuckla, Agivey and in the adjacent townlands. As someone said when some dispute arose amongst them, "all the waters in the Bann couldn't wash them separate".

My mother was an excellent scholar. She had been a monitress in the school at Drohed where she had been taught by Mr. Boyd and his sister Miss Boyd. It was a school where Protestant and Catholic were taught side by side, She always had, as she said, "the Protestant Our Father". "For thine is the power and the glory forever and ever Amen". She took it, she said; it was not rammed or forced down her throat. She liked it. Perhaps it reminded her of happier days, for, in her 60's after she had suffered a stroke, one night she began to speak very politely and to laugh at herself. "That's Master Boyd's English I speak it regular".

But to go back a few years - my father Willie John Crawford came as a young man to work as a servant man to Frank Dempsey in Drumale, Aghadowey. It wasn't very far from Kilrea and it was no distance across the Bann either. He met my mother in Drumale.

My grandmother had wanted her to marry a man of 60, no harm that he was about 40 years older than herself, since he was brave and well off. The old woman was enraged when her aunt, Mrs. Hegarty, told her to take the young'un. My grandmother and my aunt Mary Ann boycotted the wedding, and there was the greatest row at the very door of the Church at Bovagh.

Mrs. Hegarty, whom they often referred to as Katy McAnally, took the young pair in and it was at her home that John and James were born, this in a little house about three fields from the banks of the Bann.

Her sister, Jane, married James Crawford, a brother of my fathers. Two brothers married two sisters. Lizzie had been engaged to be married, the date had been set for the wedding, the best man had been arranged and the bridesmaid triced. At the last minute, I'm sure for good reason, she changed her mind and took

the road to Derry and the boat to Boston. Her family now live in an area of Massachusetts called Wrentham.

She married a jeweller, he could have been a watchmaker, he was of Portuguese origin called Maday and her daughters Mrs. Birmingham, Mrs. Pomfret and Mrs. Watterson - Alice, Margaret and Florence have kept in touch through the years. Florence's husband, William Watterson, had been taken as a babe in arms from Magherafelt to the United States by his widowed mother, she to serve her time in the cotton mills of that area and he to work there for the rest of his life.

Her brother John married in Drumale and Jamie you'll hear of again. By the time I was born my mother, father and my brothers John, Jamie and Hugh were living at the Enagh, Ballymoney. That my mother had regrets for Co. Derry I had no doubt but she didn't have too much time to dwell on them as she made ends meet, attended my father, kept up what appearances she could and set standards perhaps far above our station. She was a good woman with very definite opinions and principles. Her talents were put to full use bringing up the ten of us!

My mother, Ellen Crawford (nee Dunlop)

Above: Charlie and Mrs. McDonald (nee Dunlop)

Left: Charlie McDonald, Ellen and Maggie with their father.

Above: Ellen McDonald

Centre: Maggie McDonald

Top Right: Peggy Mitchell, grand-daughter of Charlie and Ellen McDonald

Bottom Right: John McDonald who worked for Glasgow Transport

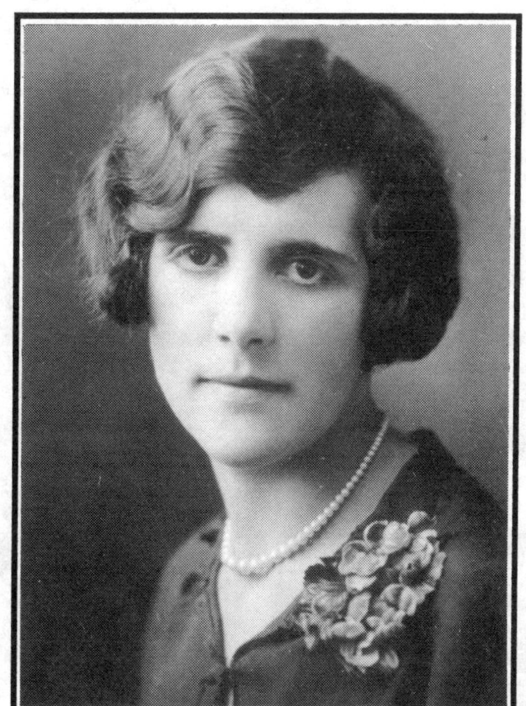

Left to Right: Alice, Florence and Margaret

Bottom Right: Mrs. McGauran (Maureen), Mrs. Birmingham (Alice), Mrs. Watterson (Florence) and Mrs. Pomfret (Margaret) in 1961

The Diamond Rasharkin

Maghera Street, Kilrea

William John Crawford with his son, Patrick, seated on his knee - still in skirts!

My Father

Next I expect I should speak of my father. My father was born on the 8 March 1865, in Magheraboy, Rasharkin. His father was James Crawford, his mother had been Ellen Jane Connelly, the daughter of Archy Connelly a shoemaker in the Movanagher district not too far from Kilrea. She was of the Church of Ireland and was reared in the Church of Ireland as were her sisters Mary Ann and Martha (Mattie) and a young brother called Jonathan Hugh, who had been a teacher in the Kilrea area but who died very young. There probably were others who died in infancy.

According to my father's tale, his father was working as a servant man to Dempseys, priests and farmers about Movanagher whom he said were relatives of his own, when he met my grandmother. She was instructed in the Catholic religion by the same priests, received into the Catholic Church and married to James Crawford.

My father was to be called William after his grandfather. His mother's people wanted him called William. His mother's younger sister carried him to Kilrea to register his birth and she registered him as John. Another version of the story was that his father was to register his birth in Kilrea but after being too well treated on the market day clean forgot what name the child was to be called. So he was registered as John. He was christened in Rasharkin Catholic Church and was known always as William John. Much later when he went to find his birth lines for the railway he found that he was not William but John, although he had been called William John all his life.

He spoke of going to a very makeshift kind of school with benches that they sat on and with an earthen floor, but he left school with only the rudiments of reading or writing, but with a great gift of the gab to the end of his days, a fund of stories, many of which I doubted but some were proved true later. He claimed descent from Robert the Bruce and I can remember my mother committing an old volume of history to which he was much attached to the flames with "Scotch wha hey how are ye?" as it went up in smoke. He extended his interest in reading in later years.

He had a brother James, a Hugh, Andy, Archy and Phonsie and one sister Liza. Hugh and Liza ended their days in Pittsburgh. Liza wrote very well from the United States. So did the girls get more education or did she learn later as a young girl in America?

Regarding my father's stories he said the Reverend Jameson, who used to drive down the Rasharkin road, and Doctor Jameson were relatives. I somehow think my great grandmother Connelly had been a Jameson - for what it's worth. His mother reared a good Catholic family, she was much more particular than his father who, he said, was not adverse to the odd swear word. I am a bit confused as to whether it was his father or grandfather who

Above: Aunt Liza (Crawford) Kennedy and Mr. T. Kennedy, Pittsburgh

Left: Hugh Crawford, seated, uncle of Mary and brother of William.

was killed in an accident with a mill stone. Certainly there was a connection with a mill in the family but how true his version was that the family had had fishing rights on the Bann at one time I do not know. I never tasted an eel nor had any benefits from the same, but the old man took pleasure in recalling such things.

When Sam Hannah Bell wanted him to record some of his memoirs for the BBC and he was in his 90's, as I am today, I put him off, saying it would tire the old man. Truth to tell I was a bit afraid of what he might say! The years since have proved many of his ramblings true. At 95, dying, crippled for many years by arthritis, his mind was as clear as it had been any day. His mother's sister, his aunt, Mary Ann the same rumoured to have carried him to Kilrea, lived in Portstewart. He used to go down to visit her. She was a Mrs. Hannah by then and she lived to 1938, dying aged 93. Her daughter was Mrs. Mc Curdy whose husband was John, a shoemaker at the Diamond in Portstewart. Jack, his son was better known on the stage in amateur theatricals and at drama festivals than at his shoemakers bench. Willie, a teacher, died early and Greta worked in the Post Office and another brother for the Post Office in Belfast. We kept great through the years. Greta died about 1963.

My father said his older relatives were buried in Drumagarner Cemetery, Kilrea, both Crawfords and Dempseys. He had it that earlier Crawfords came to that area via Co Down. I don't know. Though any land we had in my time, and that was for a very brief

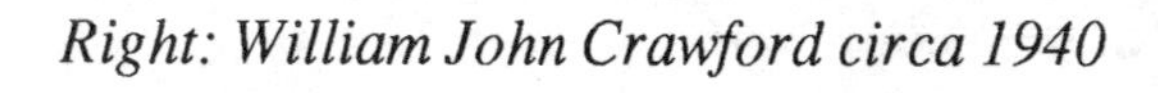

Right: William John Crawford circa 1940

"Father said the family had fishing rights on the Bann"

Right: William in his 80s

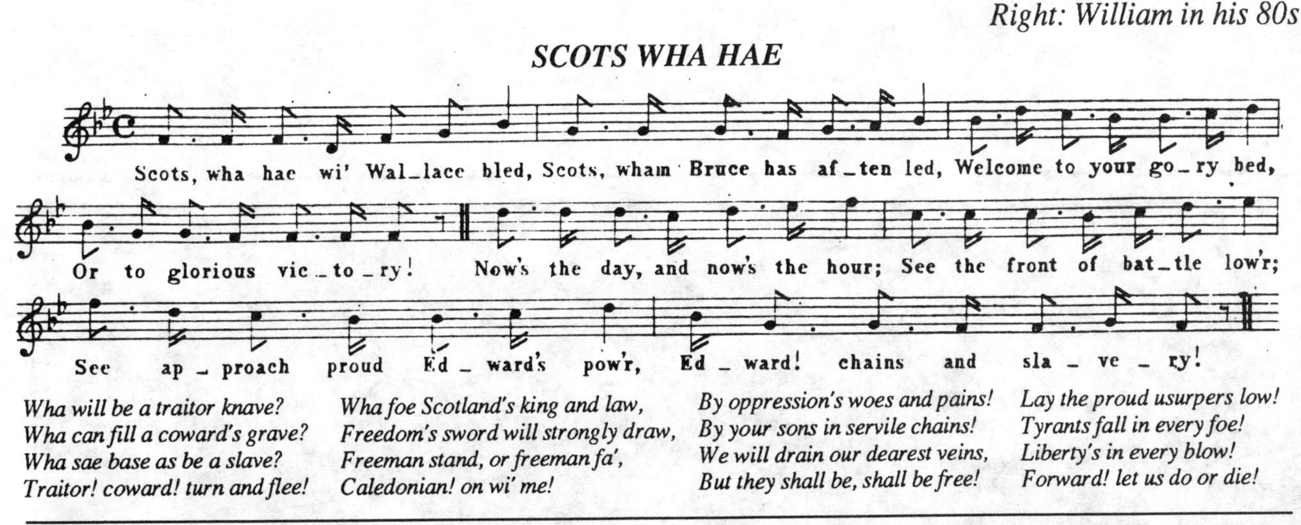

time, was very little he was preoccupied with land tenure. The O'Neills, tenant rights and Sharman Crawford, were subjects which occupied him and exasperated my mother many a time, when she would never admit she hadn't two half pennies to rub together.

When he talked of the Great Wind or when the horses and carts were driven over the frozen Bann we paid him scant attention. When he spoke of the old parish of Derrykeighan, whose roads he had travelled carting stones for James Mc Afee, we hardly listened.

Sometimes he would talk, too, of droving cattle from Kilrea to Belfast. This must have been when he was a young boy. He talked of the Alhambra and fights and broken bottles and stopping at an eating house towards the docks, near the Customs House. In later days when he might have helped Sam Hannah Bell, he and old Frank Boyle, would regale each other with endless stories for Frank's people had come from the Kilrea area and he was a born story teller and as a vet he had many tales to tell.

It is a pity such history could not have been recorded. We had no tape machines then and I suppose I am as much to blame as anyone. We often considered it old people's foibles and nonsense, and all that might have been interesting went to the graves with them.

Not that old people don't have foibles, but as I get older I am loath to admit that I have any. If I'm critical of things I'll maybe feel the years have lent me wisdom. There is no fool like an old fool.

Mary started infants school on 30th May 1899, aged 3 years 10 months.

Over the Railway Bridge to School

I was barely 4 when I started the infant school in Ballymoney - Our Lady and St. Patrick's. I suppose the walk from our house was about two miles. Did John or Jamie or Hugh take me by the hand, I can't remember being carried but I can still to this day smell the acrid smoke from the train as we crossed the Railway Bridge at Castle Street and being enveloped in a cloud of smoke. As if that was not enough, I was placed on a little form by the side of the fire and as I smelt the coal reek I was feeling sick again. I must have been a terrible crock. I felt terrible lonely. Miss Corroran turned my back to the fire and I sneaked a look every now and again to see if it was home time. I had been told how the hands would be for home. I remember Miss Corroran's surprise that I knew the orange balls on the ball frame - and me an Orange woman!

I remember afterwards rhymes about fish and fish names and colours and songs. My sister Lizzie was next to me and I can remember Miss Mc Devitt hitching up her long black elegant skirt with a tongs-like device and diving up to the gallery after Lizzie who refused to come down from her perch and giving her a quare slapping, by hand. Lizzie was very stubborn, even at that young age. I remember a wee fellow called Paddy Sheils, a nephew of the playwright, George Shiels. He was older than the rest but he couldn't see over the other scholars shoulders. He had a badly deformed back. Curiosity prompted me to touch it. He only looked round and gave me the loveliest smile and seemed pleased by the attention. He died young. The workhouse children attended school too. They were well dressed, decent and sturdy even though they wore caps as their heads had been shaved. Indeed we envied their thick cuts of bread and jam for their lunch because we only had thick pieces of soda bread and a whiskey bottle half filled with sweet milk and often times a knotted up piece of newspaper to keep it from spilling instead of a cork.

One of my earliest friends was Margaret Boyle of Market Street. Mary, another sister, later became a teacher, others were doctors. I admired and envied Margaret's long curly hair. She was that well kept and that nice she started to comb my hair and put ribbons on me. She replaced the lace which tied my hair one day with a lovely ribbon. Unfortunately the next day, minding the we'an tied by a shawl to my back before school. I slipped from a plank and I fell into a sheugh, that's the name for a kind of hollow inside the hedge filled with muck and dirt. Pulled unceremoniously out by my mother by the hair, she stabbed a hairpin from her hair into mine, gave me a clip on the ear, the stun of which I still feel, and sent me off to school. Margaret gave me many ribbons after that, she was one of my earliest school friends.

Ballymoney Boys F.C.
Front Row: C. McQuillan, A.(Phonsie) McErlain, P.McErlain, J. Sheils, P. (Ophee) Boyle;
Back row: J. Crawford, D. Mullaghan, G. McGrath, Mr. P. McQuillan, T. McDermot, S. McAfee, J. McCluskey (Banjo)

Front row: J. McGrath, C. McQuillan, P. (Feo) Boyle, J. Laverty, B. Carlin, Fr. William Byrne and Owen McQuillan centre front;
Back row: Fr. John O'Neill, S. McAfee, J. Crawford, T. McDermot, Mr. P. McQuillan, G. McGrath, J. Sheils.

Miss McDevitt was slim and elegant. Miss Corroran I admired for her training, fairness and attitudes. I felt that she had sympathy for the poor. She lived where her family had a public house and hotel on the main street and I thought she must be very rich, particularly when she took our money and got us new books from the press.

Another episode comes to mind, I wonder what the occasion was? The three schools came together and we marched round to get a pastry and a wee bag of sweets and a sixpence. Master Bradley was in charge of the boys that day. One boy I knew threw the bun up into the air as if to say "I get better than that any day". The rest of us saw few buns except perhaps Boyles, the solicitors, or Boyles the publicans, or the local R.I.C. sergeant's children, the rest of us were duly thankful for what we received.

I was always odd, I remember the examination before Confirmation when we had to stand in a semi-circle round the teachers desk. Father Farrelly came to see if we were all ready and prepared. He came from Cavan. He asked me why I was wearing that overcoat. Very reluctantly I took it off. My mother had got me a lovely dark green gym frock and a blouse. To me it was very strange and I was too shy to show it. "Don't cover that up", he said. Father Farrelly was very kind and good and concerned for the poor. Father Fullen was a curate, his father was Sir Edward Fullen who was knighted by the Pope.

One day it was 11 am by the Town Clock and I was not at school. Father Fullen met me on the main street, "You're not at school Mary?", he said. "We've another wee we'an", I said. When I got home with a few groceries he was already talking to my mother at her bedside, seeing the next addition to the family and discussing how she managed to feed us with any more than potatoes and salt (dabit the stool). I remember Cissie Quigg asking me was that man me da who was at mass with me on Sunday. She lived in Castle Street just above the fountain. (You climbed down the steps for buckets of water and the spout had a face like a gargoyle.) I was flattered to admit that he was. He cut quite a figure with his moustache clipped and his good suit on Sundays. I basked in the unexpected glory - for I was a most retiring and peculiar child, as I expect I'm an odd old woman today.

Oh! and my greatest ambition was to be in the school choir. I was tonic - solfa perfect. Moore's melodies were in my head - but I failed the test. I can still hear the class singing. "Believe me of all those endearing young charms that I gaze on so fondly today were to change by tomorrow and fleet in my arms, like fairy gifts fading away ...."

Left: Pupils of St. Patrick's School, Ballymoney 1926

Left to Right - Front row: ?, Anne McGurk, Maria McKay, Owen McQuillan, Jim Gillan, Frankie Boyle, ?, Margaret Kerr, Willie Kerr, Charlie Graham,?,Willie McConville;

Second half row: John Shields, Tommy Sheilds, ?, ?, Anne Quigg, May McKenna, Addie McKenna, Nellie Corbett, ?, Pat McConville;

Third row: Frank McKee, Dessie Henderson, Charlie McGarrell, Joe Quigg, ?, ?, Allie McCoy, Dessie Stewart, Francis McKenna, ?, Frank McKenna, Danny McKay;

Fourth row: Mary McKenna, Rhoda McKenna, Susan Daillott, Laura Laverty, Theresa Dallot, ?, Joe Shields, ? Graham, Danny Graham, Frank Lynn, Jamie Lynn, Bobbie Patterson, Ellie Shields, Willie Sheilds;

Back row : Sarah Connor?, Eileen McIlvenna, May McMullan, Maureen Gillan, Mary Alexander, Margaret McAfee?, Mary Patterson, Peggy Daillott, Anne Diamond, Rita Boyle, ?.

Ballymoney Boys 1923

MEALIE GREACHIE *(North Antrim Dish)*

coarsely ground oatmeal   *fat bacon*   *onion*

After frying some fat bacon and onion add the dry oatmeal and fry till toasted. Serve with the bacon and potatoes.
(This was made regularly by my mother in the big iron pan)

POTATO BREAD or FADGE

1lb (400g) mashed potatoes   *4ozs (100g) flour (approx)*
$^1/_2$ teaspoon salt   *1oz (25g) melted butter or margarine*

Potatoes are best used while still hot. Pile potatoes onto a floured baking board. Sprinkle with salt and melted butter. Knead in just enough flour to bind potatoes together (too much flour toughens the bread). Roll out $^1/_4$" thick or thinner if desired. Cut into farls and bake on a hot griddle or heavy pan until browned on both sides. Spread on tea towels to cool. May be eaten cold, hot buttered or fried in bacon fat served with eggs and sausages.

Note: If using leftover potatoes to which salt has been added while boiling, there is no need to add further salt.

HEARTH AND HOME

We did have a small garden, so had plenty of vegetables and potatoes and I expect a few hens. We got milk from McAfees and from Miss Wallace. My mother was a good cook and could make something tasty from nothing. She would have stripped the very hedges.

John Dempsey would bring fresh meal which they ground themselves. My mother made a dish called sowins, where she steeped the fresh meal for two or three days, then strained it, and it was like sweet cornflour when boiled. Perhaps Charlie Mc Donald would leave a small stone weight barrel of herrings. My mother would string these on sally rods at the back of the fire to smoke. She would roast them the next day on the brander and it was a wonder to me that no one choked. I didn't eat any then or fish of any description later.

All my mother's relatives were more than good. We didn't get white shop loaves in the earlier days, so my mother did as everyone else did. She made soda scones with butter- milk and wheaten scones and yellow meal farls on the open griddle. Potato bread slims, and pancakes would not be made as regularly. Flour was bought by the half hundred weight bag - the bags came in very useful with the brand names removed. I can't remember how this was done, but I can remember the soapy washing sodaey smell as they boiled. They supplied aprons, pillowcases and even sheets when four or more were opened out and stitched together.

There was no such thing as weighing the flour, the baking soda or the buttermilk. The measures were known by trial and error and the habit of years. A small tin measure served as a ladle. If the newly stoked turf fire smoked a little around the griddle it only gave an added flavour. Hunger is a good sauce.

The baking board and the goose feather to dust off the flour were in daily use.

Potatoes and cabbage were fried in the pan and were very tasty. "Kitchen" Colcannon I think you called this. Chives or finely cut spring onions were heated in a little milk and pounded into the potatoes, a hole put in the middle for the butter and if you weren't ravenous with hunger you maybe played like children at the seaside making a little castle and letting the butter run out. If you weren't so good, the pounder or beetle, when it was licked clean, was used many a time to reprimand one of us that had got out of hand. With so many of us there was many a "gorang" match and many a show of temper and many a heart scald, I'm sure, for my mother.

Sulphur and Treacle

"Are you in, Nell?" (She was never out) We'd hear this and cling to my mother's apron strings as she made her way to the roadside. Most people called my mother Ellen. Dr. McKaigney and his sister Sarah would be outside in a little pony and trap.

Dr. McKaigney was from "Co Derry", and related to my mother. He practised medicine at Kelvinside Gardens in Glasgow, and Sarah his sister acted as his housekeeper. When they were home on holiday they always stopped outside.

I can remember them handing down a three pound bag of biscuits, little iced biscuits the shape of dogs and other animals, and a big earthenware jar of jam from Rennison's shop which was at the corner of Meetinghouse Street and Seymour Street of old. Dainties for us were few.

Dr. McKaigney told my mother to dissolve lime in the drinking water and to give it to us first thing in the morning to clear the blood. He also said that nettle soup would supply iron, so my mother put on gloves and clipped nettles. It always amazed me to see the nettles turn black in the boiling water and then green again in the soup. She was also to make up sulphur and treacle in the Spring. We got a good spoonful of this each morning. I don't remember if it cleared our spots or not.

Far worse than the sulphur and treacle, even if there were grounds not mixed well enough was the "cure all" castor oil. There was always a big bottle of this high up on the dresser. It was the cure for constipation and everything else. You didn't say "no". You held your nose and swallowed it between two lots of milk.

I suffered badly from toothache and can well remember the oil of cloves which maybe eased the pain for a minute or two. A muffler would be wound round your head and neck with a sock full of warm salt wrapped inside. After a few days pacing the floor or a hope that a walk down the lane would relieve the pain there was nothing for it but the dentist's. Few of my generation had their own teeth still by thirty.

A bread poultice, white bread steeped in boiling water and a pinch of baking soda was put on a septic or festering sore to draw out the "poison". Linseed poultices were used too, for a whitlow*, or the like. Somehow I think boils are not so common today.

Epsom and Glauber salts were taken for rheumatic pains. Goose grease was saved from Christmas and rubbed on sore backs and two layers of brown paper put on top. Sloane's liniment smelled better.

** an inflammatory tumour about the nail*

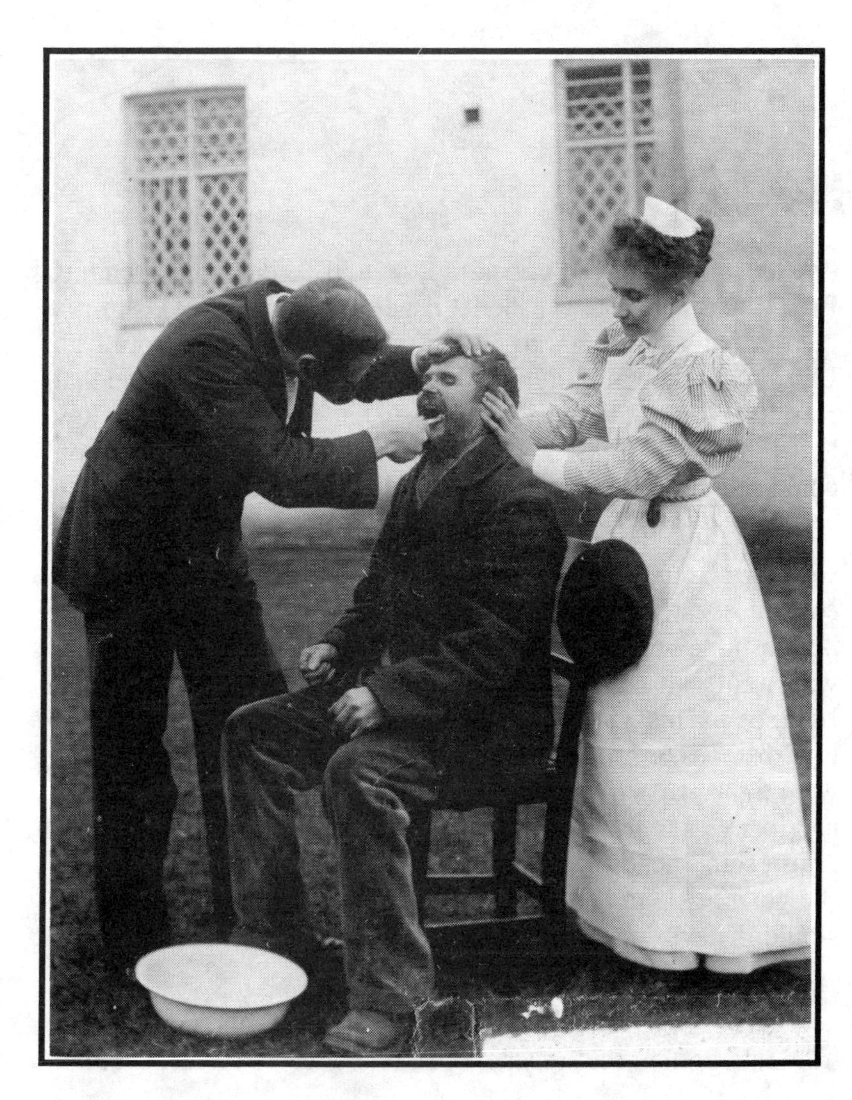

A cure for the "chin" cough or whooping cough was to be passed under the belly of an ass on the Bann Bridge. I don't remember any of us being brought. I think it would have killed you or cured you.

There was a man, Taylor, had a cure for erysipelas and there were many with cures for animals too.

Thin gruel or porridge was made for those feeling poorly, the very young and the very old. A plate of panada - white bread with warn milk and sugar was a great soother.

In those days, when whisky and brandy were cheap you'd have been given a drop of warm punch - not that I liked it then or now.

Red flannel was wrapped round me for I had a weak chest and I had long black knitted stockings and a crotched petticoat to keep in the heat. I remember often feeling poorly and taking weak turns. But calling the doctor in the very early days was a last resort and I survived.

Dr. Thompson pulling a tooth
at the Ballymoney Workhouse 1927

Over The Road

A little bit over the road from our cottage at the Enagh lived Miss Wallace. Her name was Nancy, but being well trained and brought up we seldom called her Nancy to her face. She had a wee low house and a small farm. The house is still there, in the hollow, although no connection of Nancy's has been there for (I can hardly picture it) for upwards of seventy years.

When I say I cannot picture it, I mean I cannot see how those seventy years between have slipped past. For my picture of Nancy, when I was 12 and less, is clearer than many a thing happening today.

I feel myself opening the gate opposite her house to go down the slippery field to fetch her back a three quart can of water from the well. She didn't seem to have any fear of me being run over on the road, or falling into the sunken well. How could she? I hadn't seen a motor at this time. On my way home each evening I had a little can of sweet milk to bring back.

On a Saturday evening I sat comfortably by her fireside. I expect I was glad to get away from the stir of our house to the quiet of Nancy's, where I felt important and a fuss was made of me. She would make a little tea for the two of us. Her special treat was to poach an egg on a buttered saucer, the saucer bobbing up and down on top of the big iron kettle, set to the side of the open turf fire. When that was finished I'd get a gelatin sweet from the quarter bag I'd brought to her on the Friday evening from Dan Dempsey's shop in Ballymoney. If I didn't happen to be over that particular Saturday, she always saved one for me on the window ledge. The gelatin sweets were round like a sixpence and you could see through them, a bit like jelly, but hard.

She would air her clothes for the Sabbath. Over the chair would go her petticoats all openwork and flounces that size. Her costumes, hat, gloves and shoes would be left ready. Sometimes her costume was black, sometimes steel-grey. One Sunday she wore a hat with a bow, on another, one with greeny-plush flowers, I can see and feel them yet. According to the weather she wore her lowish shoes or fine buttoned elastic sided boots. The costumes were tight-waisted with leg o' mutton sleeves. I don't mind she had many changes in my day. She always carried an umbrella, rain or shine, her bible, a handkerchief, and a gelatin sweet in case she got a tickle in her throat during the sermon in St. James'. It wouldn't have done to make a show of herself before the minister and the congregation.

After our tea Nancy would take down their family bible from the room to the fireside, open it and read a bit as I sat on a

Nancy Wallace's house

wee creepie stool by her side. Then she would say, "It's your turn Mary", and I'd open it at random and read and she would talk about holiness and behaviour and good. It was all the Bible I ever learned, and I liked it well enough.

I was very young when Nancy's sister, Sarah, died. I can remember Patrick coming up with me to the wake. Hugh wouldn't have behaved himself. We sat in the room with chairs by the walls, we didn't call it the parlour. The eight-day clock was silent on the mantle piece. I can remember the arrowroot biscuits passed around and being mortified when Patrick said, "Nancy, can I have another biscuit?" I never liked arrowroot biscuits afterwards. I was intrigued by Nancy dabbing her eyes with her handkerchief. I expect she was vexed at Sarah's death, but I had little understanding of grief at that age. I don't mind the funeral at all.

About 5 nights later, Fanny Hutchinson, a relative of Nancy's, was to stop with her. She failed to turn up and at that age I had no qualms at stopping. I said I would keep Nancy company. Into Sarah's bed I went, a four tester with curtains, as they had in those days, and soon fell asleep. When Nancy called me the next morning I couldn't answer her, the glands in my neck were swollen and I know that Miss Wallace and my mother feared T.B. for I'm sure that is what Sarah died of. I didn't stop another night. It was home to the comfort of my bed between Lizzie and Katie - two warm pelts. It was home to me no matter that the mattress or tick was stuffed with chaff and that the pillow might have been a bit hard. I wasn't so often there after that for I had odd little jobs.

Miss Wallace had friends called Archer come to visit to take tea at her scrubbed table. I never remember a tablecloth, nor do I have any recollection of the servant man who came to do work daily about her small farm and went back home in the evening on his bicycle. When she wasn't too able to care for herself she went to live with friends in Ballymoney called Merrick, in Henry Street, and when she was taken ill there, she was brought to the hospital - the Workhouse as was, now the Route Hospital, Ballymoney. I visited her once and I can remember her saying to me, "Ugh, Mary I wonder if it's true .... they say they give the old people a dose of something." Within a week Miss Wallace was dead. She is buried in St. James' churchyard, Ballymoney. May she rest in peace.

Captain James McAfee, MRCVS son of James McAfee, JP Ballybrakes, Ballymoney

Dick Mc Afee, son of James McAfee, at the old house down the lane.

Phil McAfee and Lizzie McAleece

Far right: Fr. John Healy, Administrator, St. Peter's Belfast 1911 - 1919, P.P. Loughgiel

Down The Lane

Down the lane lived the McAfees and the Healeys. We were often up and down to McAfees, even after my father had gone to work for Sam Troilland in Meetinghouse Street, and later on the railway. We grew up with the McAfees. There was usually one of each of our two families in every class in the chapel school. Sadly some of the older ones died, about the time of the bad flu, around 1915. Mary and Maggie were two of those and I remember it well. Jim was a vet in the 1st World War. John and Dick are now dead, but of John's family there is Lizzie - Mrs. Boyle, Kathleen - Mrs. McGrath and Gerald alive and Sister Margaret. Sadly Fr. Seamus, who was in the class with our Joe, died a few years ago and Nuala and Sean are also gone. Like myself, of the old family Annie and Jane soldiered on. Jane died in her 90's, not long ago.

Down the lane too, lived the Healeys. Mr. Healey had been from the west of Ireland and a Sergeant in the old R.I.C. Mary, Maggie, Joe and Fr. Healey were four of their family. Joe Healey was very interested in early photography. There were many things about the house which fascinated us. Our earliest reading, apart from school books, was from books lent to us by Healeys. They had beautiful books with plates of old flowers, shell-shaped Beleek cups, from which Daniel O'Connell drank! The beautiful table, the likes of which we never owned, was covered in the end with droppings and parrot seed. Polly was their life. The once well kept thatch fell in round their feet, the old grandfather clock came apart with damp, and Maggie and Joe grew old and died before the days of the Health Service and Social Welfare. We did what we could to help them when that time came.

To the right was Millview where Pat McKenna lived for a time, and Master McQuillan and later Becketts and Campbells live there now. From that to the Milltown, then there were no houses. To the right were the narrow fields my father once owned for a short time, now completely built up with the bungalows, narrowing to nothing at the Rasharkin Road end.

The Milltown school was to your left and at one time there must have been a kind of little village of its own. Keers, Connor and Hutchinson were common names in my day. A little row of houses ran inwards from the road and Mr. and Mrs. Kearney and Biddy lived there. Clarke's little shop was on the corner .

The old mill was on the right. This had earlier been a cornmill owned by the McElderrys. Later it was taken over by Mr. Pollock and then was a flax mill. It has had different uses since. The little river that ran under the Milltown Bridge was never a beauty spot. If I noticed the smell I hadn't time to take heed to it in the morning on my way to work, and a lot of water has run under the bridge since.

The churn, settle bed, turf and crock for the milk

My Grandmother Dunlop and Mary Ann

My Grandmother

As I've said I was born on the 12th July 1895 and John and Jamie and Hugh were born before me. Lizzie and Patrick came next. There were about two years between each of us. Katie was born in 1900 just after Christmas. From my father and mother's marriage, almost eleven years before, there had been no contact with my grandmother Dunlop or with my aunt Mary Ann.

When Katie was about to be born my mother was very ill and Mrs. Mc Afee asked if she wouldn't like her to get in touch with her people. My grandmother came. My mother and Katie survived. My grandmother came, I am told, as if nothing had happened in the interval. We were much better off after that because she brought cloth to make little pinafores for the girls and shirts for the boys. These were made from webs of cloth that could be got surplus from the shirt-making in Coleraine. Kathryn was a good seamstress and some of the patchwork quilts we still have date from these days.

The grandmother was small and sharp and quick-tempered. Mary Ann, unmarried, was what you'd call rough and ready and with no frills, but very generous, even then. She worked with the men at the brick kilns near the Bann and her hands were calloused with hard work. She was very proud of her small feet for which she had to have boots hand-made. Her bark was much worse than her bite.

Mary Ann

She wasn't over keen on hygiene or cleanliness and I can remember Patrick being indignant at the way she made bread and asking her "did you wash your hands?". I expect this was on an occasion when there was another addition to the family and Mary Ann was doing a bit to help about the house. He told her that his mother always washed her hands and wore a clean apron, "Away Paddy Blitters", she said. Strange, he was a bit like that many years later and Mary Ann didn't change over the years either - each very good in his or her own way.

After this my mother would go out to visit in "Co Derry".

I remember going out with her on the mail car; 4 a side and me in the well of the car and the shame of having to be lifted down when I got sick. I was warned by my mother to take anything my grandmother offered and not to be odd. She had killed a fowl and I couldn't eat it.

Later I went on my own for a week's holiday. Mary Ann unpacked my little bundle. "In under God what have you got here?", she asked. I'd hidden two candles for fear of the dark. "You'll sleep with the old woman", she said. I'll never forget the grunts and the groans and the "pahlin and pehlin" of the old woman, I couldn't wait for the week to be over.

Not but she was kindness itself and boiled a small three legged pot of Skerry Blues (potatoes) for me and even Jamie was polite. The house, for this was the house in which John and Jamie had been born, that they lived in by now for Jamie, or maybe it was some other one, had drunk them out of the other little farm. It was longish and low. You could see daylight up the chimney, the crane swung outwards, there was a large ash pit, two little hobs where you could sit if the fire wasn't too good and look up at the sky above. Everything was black with soot.

It was nice to sit and rock in the rocking chair that changed direction on the uneven floor. The rocking chair had worn velvet padded arms. There was an old American trunk in the corner where good linens and quilts were kept and sheets for when the dead were laid out. When Mary Ann died I found many of the things had been eaten by the moths.

Off the kitchen was a small room where Jamie slept. Down the room smelled of age and damp and neglect but there were pictures of the old people on the walls and the mantle shelf was draped with a very dusty chenille cover. There was a photograph album on the old table. The room in which I slept with Kathryn,

Extract from the Whig 1910

OBITUARY.

Mr. William M'Adorey.

The death took place yesterday of Mr. William M'Adorey, who for many years had charge of the advertising department of this newspaper. He was the oldest member of the staff, having come as a lad to serve his time in the commercial department forty-five years ago, when the "Northern Whig" office was in Callender Street, and the son of its founder, Mr. Finlay, still actively watching its interests. Ever since then he faithfully served the paper and the successive interests which owned it. For nearly forty years he was chief of the advertising department. In this capacity he came much among the commercial public, with whom his unfailing courtesy and direct manly straightforwardness rendered him deservedly popular. It would be no exaggeration to say that he made not a single enemy, while he was making troops of friends, and that during forty-five years of business life he had a good word of everybody and everybody's good word. His integrity and fidelity were recognised by those whom he served and in whose confidence he occupied a high place. By his colleagues of every grade in the "Northern Whig" office he was regarded with sincere affection, not only as the doyen of the place, but as the cheeriest, kindliest, and best of comrades. No friends, however close, will feel his loss more acutely than those who worked beside him day by day.

Mr. M'Adorey died in harness. Up to a few weeks ago he had scarcely known what illness was during his sixty years of life. Then symptoms of an internal complaint troubled him, and eventually, although he had never been laid aside for a day, it was deemed advisable that he should undergo an operation. For this purpose he went last week into the private hospital in Claremont Street, where he was under the care of Surgeon Robert Campbell and Professor Sinclair. The operation—a very severe one—was successfully performed a few days ago, but unfortunately the patient's strength gave way subsequently, and he died from heart failure yesterday morning. He leaves a widow and a family of four sons and two daughters, with whom deep sympathy will be felt in their bereavement. The funeral, as will be seen by intimation elsewhere, takes place to-morrow.

was off this. There was house-leek on the walls outside, an abundance of damsons and apples in the Autumn, crabs and others too. The hedges lining the fields going down to the Bann had red currants and black growing in between and the odd little stray crab apple tree.

I was puzzled at night when Mary Ann said we'd go up the town because we didn't go to the town, we went to the neighbouring houses. This was on her Celidhe to Hughie's Patricks or Denis' Patricks (Dempseys) or Dickson's. She'd take me to Campbell's for messages. She said if she gave money to Kathryn she'd only give it to Jamie, for she couldn't say no to him and he would only drink it.

For poaching salmon, (he had a boat at one stage) he had to go to Scotland to lie low. He was quite a character.

I remember seeing salmon and Kate Mc Afee enjoying it too, poached by Jamie and re-poached by my mother, but I never tasted it, not because of the bailiffs or anything, I just didn't savour fish nor fowl.

I never had any inclination to travel - except to the moon. I was ridiculed for saying it and yet I came to see travel to the moon in my lifetime, but Mary Ann and the grandmother would cross the Bann at the Eden to Ballymoney and travel regularly to Belfast to visit the Mc Adorey's on the Antrim Road. When Mr. Mc Adorey died, they said, the paper was edged with black, he worked on the Whig. His wife had been Dempsey. Sometimes they would get the train instead at Macfin junction.

Later Mary Ann rode a bicycle and came in on Thursdays.

The Narrow Gauge at Ballycastle Station
with H. Doherty, Guard, Ballymoney

She never missed the Lammas Fair in Ballycastle - going on the narrow gauge. She always brought back dulce and yellow-man. On Thursdays, market day, she would bring Peggy's Leg and the like to those who were still young enough to eat them.

Miss McClements had a wee sweetie shop on the Main St.

No, I never had any wanderlust in my blood. I wonder what I missed, the Golden Gate seemed very far away, Pittsburgh or Los Angeles or Vancouver - all of which I had the chance to see.

I don't suppose Peggy's Leg is sold any more. It was a soft ridged stick of confection with the flavour of cinnamon, unlike the odd rock you brought back from Portrush or Ballycastle. It was soft and easy to bite and finished too soon!

Left: Frank Boyle, MRCVS and Father Pat.

Middle: Mrs. McNabb (Mary Boyle), sister of Father Pat and Frank.

Top right: Father Pat Boyle, later Rev. Canon Patrick Boyle.
Born 16th April 1863. Ordained 12th June 1887. P.P. of Derriaghy 1907 - 1955;
The Rock, Hannahstown and St. Teresa's, Belfast. Died 10th June 1955.

Bottom right: Jeannie Boyle, another sister.

Boyles' Public House

I suppose I was about 12 when I first went to work in Boyle's. They had a public house on the corner of Main Street and Castle Street. The shop window was on the Castle Street side and the hall door was on Main Street. I used to go to help after school.

Mrs. Boyle's daughter, Mary, had been a nurse and married a Doctor Mc Nabb. She came from Castlewellan with her two children, Maureen 4 1/2 and John Joseph 2, to stop for a holiday. I went to wheel them out in their prams, but stayed on.

Mrs. Boyle had had a stroke. It was left to me to fix her to go down to mass each morning. I enjoyed fixing her cloak, putting down her little veil on a stormy day, hooking her buttoned boots, closing her gloves, handing her her prayer book. I watched her as she went down Castle Street, taking a look out. She was a tidy old lady and the nearest thing I had to a doll.

When all was quiet I'd steal upstairs to the drawing room to play the piano and act out my fantasies. To me all this was luxury and I lived in another world.

Mrs. Boyle always praised me. I was grateful for the praise and I couldn't fix her up enough.

When Fr. Pat, her son, was coming for a holiday she would put new pale blue satin material behind Our Lady's statue in his room and give me the remnants for my hair, telling me "put that in your hair - it'll be nice". If Mrs. Boyle appreciated my ministrations, Fr. Pat wasn't quite so sure - I remember him looking askance as to how I was washing the dishes. Frank, who was then training to be a vet, just winked at me behind his back.

Coming home from daily mass, Mrs. Boyle often brought 2 other ladies in for a glass of punch. She didn't take any herself - it is likely because of the stroke. This particular morning there were two rowdy, noisy types of women in the bar. One pulled off Mrs. Boyles pinz-nez, little glasses she wore on a chain - they broke on the flagged stone floor of the bar. I expected they would never set foot in the bar again, but they did, and Mrs. Boyle was as pleasant as ever.

One night her daughter Sarah was going to a dance and I was to stay to keep her mother company. Mrs. Boyle and I knelt down to say the Rosary. "Thou oh Lord will open my lips and my tongue shall announce thy praise." With that I heard the clang of the shutters on the shop window as Charlie Dallat shot the bolts. He came over every night to close up the shop. I sprang from my knees and was out the door and home in time to join my mother and father and the rest in finishing the Rosary at our own fireside. There were no recriminations at home, only Sarah saying the next morning, "Ye scut ye, going and leaving my mother like that."

Main Street, Ballymoney

Castle Street, Ballymoney

Church Street, Ballymoney

M. Cunningham, Family Grocer, Ballymoney

Before the Singer Sewing Machine

If feeding us was a problem; keeping the clothes on our backs was almost as difficult. Any sewing was done by hand. Where my mother came from they were used to sewing, what with the Bleach Green at Aghadowey and the Shirt-making in Coleraine. With an ever growing family there was a crying out need for blouses and pinafores, coats and trousers. My mother, and my father, would not have wanted anyone of us to be shamed.

Mrs. Shaw and Jeannie lived at the head of the town near the Market Square. Mrs. Shaw dealt in second hand clothes. My mother would walk into the town, though not very often and see Mrs. Shaw. She knew all our ages and sizes and would save anything she thought might suit one of us, and send it out to my mother. To this day I remember a little blue coat with brass buttons which fitted Willie, with his fair curls and much frailer build than the other boys, to absolute perfection. Mrs. Shaw was paid. We, I expect, showed a fair face to the world of Ballymoney, and there was no question of "charity", of which my mother had a fear all her life.

Late into the night and into the early hours of the next morning we would hear the clatter of scissors on the kitchen floor - the odd rattle of a cup as my father threaded needles and made cups of tea for my mother and himself as she worked through the night.

Bigger trousers were cut down and new small ones were made. Braces, or gallouses as they were called, were made for the boys. My mother doubled strips of flour bag; over stitched and over stitched the strips by hand before making the buttonholes on the ends. She wasn't satisfied to make simple little shirts or pinafores from the apron cloth she got from "Co Derry". A little contrasting collar was made for the shirts, a ruff or a flounce for the girls pinafores. My mother was more than well-doing and in this day and age would get a prize for housewifery.

The old man and old woman were both very hard-working (I don't suppose they were old then) and well-doing. Living now in the town land of Ballybrakes, (1910) only round the bend of the road from the Enagh where I was born and where Nancy Wallace had lived, there was a large garden for potatoes and vegetables of all-kinds. At times we had a couple of cows and pigs, hens and ducks.

By this time, although we had got one of the new labourer's cottages, my father was no longer a farm labourer. He went from Sam Trollands in Meeting house Street to work on the "Permanent Way" on the railway. He helped lay the 'new' Derry Central line. Because he was not a farm labourer any more he had to pay half-a-crown in rental to the council instead of one shilling and sixpence. The Hannahs who were Town Clerks were relatives of his own.

About the time John, the eldest of the family, started serving his time to the tailoring in H Mc Curdy Hamilton's, in 1910, an old sewing machine was purchased. John would have done some sewing at home. I was observant enough, I saw John wax ball the thread and tailor tack. I saw how he measured and marked with tailor's chalk. I watched him, cross-legged, sewing, steam pressing with his heavy "goose" iron. In the earlier days the irons for the box iron had been heated in the fire and taken out with the tongs. Later the small irons and the goose were heated on top of the range. When the spit jumped off the iron it was warm enough to press the lapels of a man's black serge suit. It was in the days before the Fifty Shilling Tailors and a man was lucky to have one good suit for wakes and weddings, Chapel or Church on Sundays.

Jamie was soon working and Hugh was out of work of'ner than in. By the time I brought home my first pay from McElderrys on a Thursday my mother felt she was so well off she'd think of going off to America for a holiday.

Tailor's Group, H. McCurdy Hamiltons circa 1910
(John in cap and braces)

THE TECH

Hugh, Lizzie, Kate and myself all went to night classes at the Tech. Mr. Pettigrew was the headmaster. He said the chapel school sent pupils who were very good at writing and spelling but not so good at mathematics. Long practice made me very good at mathematics. We got an excellent training in commercial subjects but had little chance to use typing or short-hand later.

Cookery and house craft stood us in good stead from the days we attended the Tech. In the cookery room were rows of scrubbed white tables, pot stands, yellow earthenware bowls, wooden spoons, wire sieves, black ranges and gas cookers. There were pulleys overhead to hold our starched garments on the nights we were taught how to fold and iron a tablecloth or the order of procedure in ironing a man's shirt.

Mr. Pettigrew was one of the first to encourage George Shiels in his playwriting. Many a young man had his first lessons in a craft which he would follow for the rest of his life, about Ballymoney or even Vancouver.

Technical Schools, Ballymoney

Above: John and Willie
Centre: (Mrs) Kathleen Crawford, James and Mary circa 1920
Top right: Lizzie
Bottom right: Katie

Our Family Bible

These are the names of the family, recorded in the Bible, which was given by my Grandmother Crawford along with the American clock to each of her married sons.

Names and dates of birth:

John Crawford	**15/1/1890**
James Crawford	**3/8/1891**
Hugh Crawford	**14/5/1893**
Mary Crawford	**12/7/1895**
Lizzie Crawford	**20/4/1897**
Patrick Crawford	**13/2/1899**
Katie Ann Crawford	**28/12/1900**
William Crawford	**10/9/1902**
Andrew Gerard Crawford	**11/1/1905**
Joseph Columba Crawford	**5/3/1908**

I don't need either of my two pairs of glasses to remind myself of any of them. Of the 10 recorded only Andy, Joseph and myself remain, the last one to go was Katie.

JOHN

John, the eldest , was full of fun, social and amiable, given to pulling your leg; though not I suppose in a cruel way. He loved circuses, plays and music-hall turns in the Parochial Hall. He loved John Mc Cormack and he loved opera records on the first old gramophone. He had many friends, not only amongst the tailors in Hamilton's, but among the young men playing pitch and toss at the Recess on the road, the beggars and callers, and the old people in the Milltown. Never a Christmas passed from he began working that he did not make up Christmas boxes for some of those more needy than ourselves - it might have been a plug of tobacco and a noggin of whiskey for one, a packet of tea and sugar for another. Most Saturday afternoons (his half-day from Hamilton's) Dummy Mearns came with him. It was the custom in those days for trades such as tailoring to employ the deaf handicapped. John conversed fluently with him in the deaf and dumb sign language. John would come home with a creamy cottage rose cutting he had got from one of the other tailors, or a bunch of special velvety-purple pansies behind his back. One hot July Saturday, he was just 53, he collapsed and died at the Milltown wall on his way home.

Hugh
who died in France during the Great War on 4th April 1918

Andy in Los Angeles, late 1920s.

Patrick in Los Angeles, also late 1920s

(These two photos were taken in the same studio used by Clarke Gable and other early movie stars).

JAMIE

Jamie, next to John in age, may have been a little in his shadow. He was quiet and thoughtful. In his twenties he went to work in the Shale mines about Livingstone station, near Edinburgh. He returned to spend the rest of his life, until retirement, at the station in Ballymoney. It was he who went with John to a football match in Dublin. Over the weekend they both met an elderly man and two of his relatives in Glasnevin cemetery. John, as usual, got into conversation with this old man. They were entertained at his home in the centre of Dublin, John in his element with his family and the relative from Mayo and her young niece. But it was Jamie who married the woman from Mayo - the only one of the family to marry! He died in Newcastle, Co. Down on St. Patrick's Day 1966, aged 74.

HUGH

Hugh was the most likable and unbiddable of the whole family. All his life he was in danger of being shot instead of the crows, or drowned in the Layde or the Bann for that matter. He had many friends, both Catholic and Protestant. He played football. Finding sitting on an office stool in Boyle's office training to be a Solicitor's clerk was far too frustrating he took off to Scotland to join Jamie and from there he enlisted in the 1st World War. He died in France, 4 April 1918, aged 24. My mother never really recovered from the shock and it marked all our lives.

LIZZIE

Lizzie was fairish-auburn haired. In the present day she might have received a good education. She went to Irish classes at night. She would have liked to have been a nun. As it was, she worked in the Refreshment Rooms at Ballymoney and Ballymena stations but spent the greater part of her life keeping house. She died in the Mater Hospital aged 50.

PATRICK

Patrick worked for a short spell at the railway and then for the O'Boyles in their spirit grocers in Nelson Street, Belfast. The owner was shot at his own door in the "Troubles". Patrick returned to Ballymoney for a spell and he worked in Nestle's Creamery in Meeting House Street. He was inclined to be asthmatic and when he emigrated in 1923, it was hoped the climate of Los Angeles would be healthier for him. He worked there for Carnation Creameries for the rest of his life. He corresponded regularly through the years and never a birthday or Christmas was forgotten. In late years he returned home a few times but died suddenly in Los Angeles in 1966; about 3 months after Jamie died in Newcastle, Co. Down, aged 67.

KATIE

Katie, I always felt, had somehow inherited something of the grandmother Dunlop who came to attend her birth. She was very thin with dark skin and dark brown eyes. Both of us received the same commercial training and she was very good, and a

"The parents of Lance Corporal (acting Sergeant) Hugh Crawford, H.A.I; M.G.S; who reside at Ballybrakes, Ballymoney, received on Saturday last the Military Medal awarded their son, who fell in action on 4th April 1918. This gallant soldier was one of the finest men to enlist at the outbreak of war....."

Above:Patrick on his way to America on the upper deck of the HF Alexender.

Left: O'Boyle's Spirit Grocers where Patrick worked.

beautiful writer. But she hadn't the same enthusiasm for serving people as I had. Nothing pleased her better than a detective story and a packet of Woodbines. Shortly after retirement she returned from Ballymoney having posted a letter, collected the papers in Friels and changed her library books, sat down in the chair at the side of the fire and died, aged 68.

WILLIAM

William was shorter than the other boys and much fairer with light brown wavy hair. He was particularly good with his hands and loved carpentry. Sadly he got T.B. and in those days there was no cure. He lingered for a while. In those days, too, there was a financial strain in looking after the sick at home, besides the sadness of seeing them fade away. I can remember Willie had a lovely little pomeranian dog to which he was very attached. When Willie was confined to bed we felt it wasn't fair to him or the little dog to have it jumping up on to the bed. We took it a distance to a good home but it made its way back. On a sad day in November 1937 when the snow was shoulder high and a trench had to be dug to walk along, Willie was buried, aged 35.

So Andy, Joe and myself are left. Andy wouldn't have much sympathy with my reminiscences, so I'll respect him and keep my silence. Joe might not mind, though he can be determined enough in his own way. Anyhow the old American clock, the replica of those given by my grandmother Crawford to her sons Archy and Phonsie, has just struck five and Andy wants to check his pools in the hope that we will die rich!

HE whom this scroll commemorates was numbered among those who, at the call of King and Country, left all that was dear to them, endured hardness, faced danger, and finally passed out of the sight of men by the path of duty and self-sacrifice, giving up their own lives that others might live in freedom.

Let those who come after see to it that his name be not forgotten.

L/Cpl. Hugh Crawford, M.M.
Machine Gun Corps (Cavalry)

Above: The Old Workhouse, now the Route Hospital.

Right: Gate End Clearance Area, 1958.
Front of houses nos. 22,24,26,28,30 and 32 Gate End.

Pride, Poverty, Land and Property

"The Lord preserve us from any of ye dying before we've the money to bury ye." This was a real and constant dread for my mother as we grew up, when nearly every family lost young ones with diptheria, scarlet fever, whooping cough and meningitis. This was something, I suppose, she had to face. Others died from sheer weakness and want. What was called "decline" later was openly called tuberculosis or T.B. There was no remedy and it spread like wildfire through a whole family. I knew as many as six young people in a big family die, one after the other in the early days of the century, and we knew it ourselves. It was a scourge.

"Hear ye, hear ye!"

When I was in Boyle's in the early 1900's a man called McGahey was the town crier. He'd be going along the street with his sandwich boards and bell. The sign might be a sale notice or an announcement of a music hall event. Duffy's circus put out their own bills and the beggars had their own little penny song sheets.

Sadly part of his job was to collect when someone died without the family having the wherewithal to bury him or her. To be buried as a pauper was a terrible disgrace. When these house to house collections were made we gave what we could. I'd have followed him step by step to the town clock as he went from door to door. For someone as odd and retiring as I was, I must have had a strong streak of curiosity. Families well off today, more power to them, went through things like this. We came through without this but I feel my mother shouldn't have dreaded it so.

Among my friends in early school days was another Mary. Mary and her two brothers had been abandoned by the roadside as infants. The police took them to the Workhouse. I think it was about the Ballymena Line they were found huddled under the hedge.

From the little medals pinned on the children's clothes it was known they were Catholics, but their names were not known. Mary told me later the name she bore was of a famous Donegal clan. So it was, but when it came to naming her in the Workhouse, there was a nurse who had cared for the three little waifs and it was her name they were given. I know because the nurse had a brother a priest and they used to visit my mother.

Mary bore this name honourably, if not to her grave - for she married afterwards. When one of her brothers, who went into service with a Protestant farmer died later, she insisted on repaying this same farmer for his burial. Mary had no children. I don't know what happened to her other brother. She was as decent a wee soul as ever walked.

Many years later on a dark winter's night their mother rapped at Mary Connor's (Mrs. John McKees) door on the Ballymena Line. John McKee brought her in and gave her tea. She wanted to make contact with Mary, but Mary didn't want it.

Mary Connor was a friend from school until the day she died. They lived in Castle Street. Mrs. Connor had been from Loughgiel, a fine woman in every way. Work was hard got for Johnny, and, Mrs. Connor worked all her days. I remember her telling me that after she married and was pregnant with Mary she was working for a pork butcher and his wife and family. Work was hard. The little tin which the mistress gave her with a grain of tea to make tea for herself was small. Mary was expected. One day Mrs. D. told her she didn't need her any more for "The Master doesn't like to see you like that."

Annie Connor was younger than Mary. She married Willie Cairns. She died leaving a young son who is dead now as well as Annie. Mary and John McKee had two children, Kathleen and Francis. I was very fond of them as children, and was God-mother to Kathleen and many more.

They were not the good old days. How could they be when the rich looked down on the poor, when people lived in penury and want. I loved children but having and rearing them was the lot of the mother. It was expected that the woman dance attendance on the menfolk.

There was a different rule for the poor wee girl left with a baby to rear. Where a grandmother accepted the child was an exception rather than the rule, I never believed, or was allowed to believe in too much freedom but I had only pity for the many I knew through the years left in such circumstances.

It must have been in the 30's when I read in "Thompson's Weekly" of a little girl, without mother or father looking for a home. I would have dearly loved to have adopted wee Teresa and given her a home and coddled her and cookered her. I don't think I would have spoiled her. Even now I love children and to see them. And they say an old maid's children are always perfect.

You went in awe and were ill at ease with your 'betters'. I remember Dr. Boyd being very off-putting to me as a child, with his half-castor hat, cuff-links and all. Hugh had come with me to the Dispensary and Dr. Boyd had gone into the back to make up a bottle of medicine for me. When I asked if I'd have to go to school the rest of the week he said "No, you can stay off", and actually smiled. So he was human after all. Its good that times have changed and that there are people to care about the working class. In my earlier days the poor had no rights. In this day and age anyone can become anything. There were no trade unions then to work for fair employment . . . I thought you had switched that off.

The old man's wish to own land of his own never deserted him. After Hugh's death (R.I.P.) and with Hugh's war pension he was able to buy the point of land towards the Rasharkin Road end and another field up the Rasharkin Road. He would have had a horse in the upper field, the grazing in the others was poor but he could walk a field and know it was his own. The point was sold later to R.A. McElderry and was soon developed as building land - it's completely built up today.

As for the property this was a few little houses in Castle Street at Gate End just below McArthur's shop. Rents from the same were small and it came to the stage where repairs required to the same were beyond his means. They were just passed over to the tenants.

We were not meant to be rich.

Fair Day, Ballymoney, late 19th/ early 20th century. Ballymoney was often referred to as "Cowtown"!

The Broad Stone

Going to the Broad Stone was like going to Cork today. In the early days we might have gone on the back of a ruck shifter. Richard McAfee lived up that way about the Knockans and my father would have been up working at hay or the like. We might have had an outing in a pony and trap. Later I would have ridden a bicycle. It was hard peddling up the Rasharkin Road, past Alcorn's the photographer's and Sam Kane's, the tailor's and Moores lane to the right. Further to the left was The Braod Stone near Finvoy.

It was a place apart, quiet but for the drone of bees on a Summer's day. There was no disturbance from the chieftain, or whoever slept there. It was a peaceful place.

I visited my grandmother Crawford in Rasharkin, before she died in 1918, about the same year in which my grandmother Dunlop died. She was propped up in bed and well able to talk to me. On her quilt she had a conglomeration of prayer beads - I remember her explaining to me the little blue dolour beads, with the stories of Mary's sorrows on the medals between. Over the bed were pictures of Our Lady of Perpetual Succour and Our Lady of Sorrows and many more. She was at pains to tell me she had not lost conceit in the Catholic religion. Well she had been a Catholic longer than a Protestant. When she died in 1918 I got a lift up in Baxter's "cart". My Aunt Liza wrote from Pittsburgh to "her dear brother William" with sorrow that she could not have been there when "their dear mother" died.

Past the Whinny Hill and in to the left was where my uncle Jamie Crawford lived. He had married my aunt Jane Dunlop and they lived at Lisheehan. Jimmy (who went to Scotland), Andy, Hugh and Paddy were sons. Mary Ann (later Mrs. Conroy in Pittsburgh), Katie (Mrs. Goldie in Glasgow), Ellen (Mrs. Joe Mc Kinney) who minded her grand-aunt and ours, Mary Ann (Mrs. Hannah) in Portstewart were daughters. These were our first cousins, doubly related. Of course my uncles Archy, Andy and Phonsie are long gone and Hugh in Pittsburgh too. Of the next generation of Crawfords only Andy, Joe and myself survive in Ballymoney, Bella Crawford (Mrs. Hugh Mullan) and Rose Crawford are in Rasharkin, Katie Dunlop (Mrs. Gowdy) lives at Ligoniel, Belfast and Hugh's daughter (Mary Crawford - Mrs. Ward) lives in Michigan. Of the next generations of Crawfords there are so many I've long lost count.

The Uncle Jamie was small and lightly built. You would hardly have arrived in Lisheehan than he would have been taking out his pocket watch. It wasn't that he was inhospitable and it wasn't fear that the police would have been after you if you hadn't

Broadstone Cromlech, Craigs, Ballymoney.
The Green Collection

a light in the old carbide lamp on the bicycle. Old Jamie played the violin and Phonsie even made fiddles. But although we loved music and singing and certainly had the taste for it I can't say any one of us excelled beyond the Jews harp and the mouth organ, or my attempt by ear at "The Last Rose of Summer" on Boyle's piano of old.

Milltown Mill (1915) McElderry & Pollock

Top row: *Wm. Murdock, Jas. Getty, John Biggart, Danny Dillon, Matthew O'Neill, Tom McAllister, Wm. Stewart*

2nd row: *Wm. MacAfee, Robt. MacAfee, Wm. Darragh, Sam Elliot, John Moore, Wm. Keers*

3rd row: *Robt. J. Hutchinson, Misses K. Crawford, E. Wilson, K. Wilson*

Front row: *Miss Mgt McDonald, Miss M. Beckett, R.A. McElderry, W.C. Pollack, Miss Nina Murdock, Bertie Stinson.*

FROM BALLYBRAKES TO McELDERRY'S

I began working for R.A. McElderry in 1918. I had left the house every morning by 6.30 am, my mother would have been up and had the lamps lit. In the early days I walked, in the later years I had a bicycle. Down the road I went past the Milltown and up towards the Railway Bridge, along Gate End and Castle Street, round the corner past Boyles and up the Main Street past the Diamond. Then it was across Linenhall Street to Market Street and the Weigh Bridge to my place of work for 37 years. This was my daily routine every day but Sunday. Every morning it was past the Milltown Mill and Clarke's wee shop and across the Railway Bridge, I knocked up the McMasters and Bairds because alarm clocks in those days were few and far between. There was a little sweetie shop belonging to Mc Arthurs on the left hand side of the street. (K. McArthur was a local athlete who won the marathon race in the Olympic games in Stockholm in 1912.) I had passed Graham's, who still made tin cans and the little old houses which were white-washed with half doors, thatched roofs and steps up to the door. Corbetts and Kirkwoods lived there.

The Lavertys lived nearby, the old man Jamie Laverty had been a tailor and there was a big family. Mrs. Laverty only died some years ago about as old as I am today, indeed I think she was nearer the hundred. I'll not make it

To the right and near the pump lived Mrs. Boorman. She might have been out early in the morning filling a bucket of water at the pump for she went to early Mass every day. You climbed down the steps into her house where there was always smoke

McKay, Townhead Street, Blacksmith.

Group at McElderry's about 1920. Mr. R.A.McElderry on running board of "new" Chevrolet van. Mary Crawford 3rd from right.

wafting out over the half-door and she was always black with smoke and so was the house, because there was many an evening I used to go in and sit with her.

I passed the chapel gates making the Sign of the Cross and I'm sure saying a very brief prayer, I wasn't what you would call Gospel-greedy. I passed Pollocks, the grocers in Castle Street and Sleepy Valley where the houses were at the back of an alley way and went past Dalatts on the right. The brothers were carpenters and coffin makers, Angelo McAfee made head stones near the fountain. I'd passed the blacksmith's McKays on the right, though it was too early yet for them to be up shoeing the horses or to hear the hammer on the anvil.

On the left I passed Cairns lodging house where the homeless and the beggars and the social misfits of that day found a bed for the night. This was before the social benefits of today. How many pennies they paid a night to Maggie and Mary Anne, I don't know. Often of an evening you heard fighting and a drunken row, but at this time of the morning all was quiet and peaceful. I turned Boyle's corner past Friel's shop on the right. Ahead of me I could see the town clock at the top of the hill coming towards seven, but I was never late. When I came to the Diamond I would think of the old music hall song "Down in Ballymoney in the Old Town Hall", but I thought far more of the ghosts of those people of '98 who had been killed at the Diamond and whose bones had been dug up later when they were building a new road or digging a sewer.

I had passed Bloody Hutchinson's stamping ground. He had been a solicitor and magistrate back about the '98 rebellion and a cruel one at that. Children misbehaving in Ballymoney were threatened with him and told Bloody Hutchinson would get them. In the mists of a winter morning he might have lingered beyond midnight. My imagination was always good, so good that I sometimes frightened myself. At last I crossed High Street and went along Linenhall Street and was nearly there, past the Weigh Bridge to the gate with the keys to the yard to open up for the carts and the shop. How many times was this routine repeated? I never thought to count them.

Bloody Hutchinson's house next to Youngs hardware shop.

Left:Tommy Rock

Right:Bobbie Moore

The Weigh Bridge

The Weigh Bridge was just to the left of Mc Elderry's yard gate. I look back to McElderry's with a happy feeling. To me R.A. was a kind, polite and courteous employer - a gentleman. The McElderrys had come from Leitrim, about Kilraughts. This was the older people. They always had had to do with the markets in Ballymoney. Two of the older generation settled in Ballymoney. One brother settled in Charles Street and the other in Victoria Street. When he was 15 he had to leave Belfast Royal Academy to come home to run the market business because of his father's illness.

I knew this because when I had occasion to leave keys, ledgers or the like to Charles Street of an evening, he would speak to me of the origins of his family, of '98 and pikes in the thatch at the Topp in the old home and tell me of all the people in the photographs in the drawing room, many of whom were doctors and missionaries in far off places.

When I went to McElderry's in 1918, there was not a shop as such. There had been flax and pork markets for many years. This was in the days when flax was brought on a Wednesday and pork on a Thursday. It was in the time when all farm produce was brought to the town, when on a market day, pig carcasses in carts, covered by a white sheet was a common sight and cattle being driven along the streets, running amok on the footpaths and into doorways was part of the exciting life of Ballymoney.

Bruce Wallace came as manager to establish a small grocery business. His father had had a shop in Linenhall Street and this is were he learnt all about shopkeeping. In the beginning this was just trade in flour, feeding stuffs for animals, tea, sugar and the like. This trade grew to what was for me a lovely shop with 2 proper counters, a till, a series of drawers for pepper, spices, cloves, nutmegs, caraway seeds and laces.

You bagged sugar and tea and peas and lentils, buff coloured bags for some, grey-blue for others. I was adept at tying parcels and making knots. I took pride in my expertise and I liked people.

While the flax markets were still in operation I kept the accounts and knew many of the flax-buyers, Mr. Magowan, whose son later taught French in Dalriada, Mr. McCombe, Mr. McMaster and Paddy Cassidy who represented Hamill of Trench House in Belfast. I was not particularly knowledgeable about flax, apart from my stomach turning at the smell of flax "retting" in the dams. My hands were too frail for the labour of pulling flax. In hard times we had done some flowering on linen, white linen work given out on a piece system and worked at night by very

Pulling and tying flax - a common scene around Ballymoney. The Green Collection

poor light for pennies. I was a good writer, speller and counter - I was never good at sewing or the like, I hadn't patience for it.

As it was, I kept the flax accounts well, enjoyed the commotion and talk. When the market was over the men resorted to one of the many pubs, there was Boyle's in Market Street - the same Boyle's whose Margaret took me in tow at the Chapel school and gave me a ribbon for my hair. Margaret gave piano lessons. I knew Charlie better then, as others of the family had left Ballymoney. McErleans was nearby and McCormacks on the corner. At that time there were 26 public houses in Ballymoney.

Part of my job in the early days was to attend the van men. In the market yard at the back of the shop the motor vans lined up in the alcoves which earlier had been stables for horses. There were seven vans in all, five served the Ballymoney area and two came from Castlerock twice a week. Mr. McElderry was the first exporter of graded eggs to the English market. The carts were stocked and orders were left for me.

Each night the van men came in late and it was my job to fill the orders for tea and sugar, tobacco and the like. The large drawers took a 14lb bag of flour. The van men collected the eggs from the farms. This dealing was mainly done with the farmers' wives. The van men had a little trade on the side. They would deliver newspapers, if it was the Whig or the Irish News, it arrived a little late, if it was the Chronicle or Constitution it didn't matter since they had a week to read it, if it was Old Moore's Almanac, there was a year ahead. And if it was an inside shirt or a pair of drawers for an old man, it was hoped he'd last the snows of another winter.

I checked out my columns of "out" and "in", charged up the money, marked out and squared up. Each book was done before 10 am and the "carts" should have been on the road before 12.00 to Armoy, Loughgiel, Finvoy and Rasharkin, Agivey and Aghadowey.

Hugh Coulter, Willie Sterling, Tommy Rock, Davy Dunlop, Adam Todd, Andy Madden and Tommy Lyness have been long off the road, but with me they are still alive.

The years passed after the first World War. Bob McAfee was later manager and also owned the Route Cafe opposite the market. (He was J.P. and Grandmaster of the Orange Order in N. Antrim). Each day I had lunch in the cafe. Jennie McAfee marked my birthday with a lovely butter sponge cake with fresh cream and peaches between, and a bunch of orange lilies. "Hmm!"

Butter and even margarine was cut from a slab. Tea of different grades came in tea chests. One was always in demand as a safety pen for the child in the days of open fires and pots of boiling clothes lifted onto the kitchen floor.

I took pride in the way I tapped down the bags of tea or sugar or flour or beans or peas or rice or lentils, folded the sides neatly over and the flaps to the middle. There was satisfaction in rolling out the twine from the ball on the wooden counter to tie a knot at the top and breaking off the string.

I never ate bacon but I loved to see the neat slices of pale or smoked coming off the slicer. For me there was an art which I suppose became a habit in the way I put a double fold in the greaseproof paper and then wrapped the parcel in brown paper

ADULT'S FOOD RATION FOR A WEEK

R.B.1
10 MINISTRY OF FOOD 1
RATION BOOK
(GENERAL) 1947-1948
Surname CRAWFORD
Initials Mary NATIONAL REGISTRATION NUMBER UASR 531 : 3
Address (as on Identity Card) Ballybrakes Ballymoney
(For change of address)
FOOD OFFICE CODE No.
M.o.F. N.I.1
BALLYMONEY FOOD OFFICE
IF FOUND RETURN TO ANY FOOD OFFICE
Serial No. of Ration Book M 881687

Meat *8oz*
Tea *2oz*
Butter *2oz*
Bacon *OR*
Ham *4oz*
Jam *OR*
Marmalade *2oz*
Margarine *2oz*
Lard *2oz*
Suet *20z*
Eggs .... *sometimes 2 per week, often just 2 per month*
Cheese .... *1oz, or slightly more according to availability*
Milk .... *fluctuated between half pint and two pints*
Dried Milk ..... *one tin per month*
Sugar *12oz*
Dried Eggs ..... *one packet every eight weeks*
Bread *and*
Flour .... *nine units per week (one unit equals 7oz)*

Some other foodstuffs, like **Chocolate** *and* **Sweets** *were on coupons and worked out around 3 to 4oz per week*

The Ministry of Food also controlled the issue of **Soap** *at around 4oz per month per person*

The use of **Gas, Electricity, Coal, Light** *and* **Water** *supplies was also curtailed. Only one third of the population possessed driving licences during the war and most of those were for commercial vehicles.*

and tied it with string.

Even cutting a plug of tobacco pleased me or changing the carbon in the book for the next order. Above all I liked people.

In these years there was variety, biscuits were mainly loose in open containers most tempting for children. Broken ones were a Godsend to the poor and there were plenty of those. So too were bacon cuttings, and eggs which had been cracked. I always did what I could for the old and poor. In the pre-war days we didn't have too many tinned stuffs.

When unemployment was rife and old age pensions still below 10/=, every little helped. Sixpence bought the makings of a dinner. Bob McAfee indeed did many acts of kindness for the callers at the shop in those days, but, as a Catholic, I was well aware of being a minority and always stood up against discrimination as best I could. I always believed in standing up for what was right.

Even in a small town, and perhaps even more because of it, you could not help but be aware of the attitude towards those of us in more menial positions. Like many another, I was awed by a fancy hat, fox-fur with beady eyes, a large hand-bag, a dab of rouge and a waft of perfume, "Evening in Paris", or another. Not but I was treated as an equal by many of the "better" class and was the confidant of many.

The message boys delivered groceries. A large order deserved a little bag of sweets. At Christmas time there was a festive feeling about the muscatels and cherries and plums for the Christmas puddings and the cut glass bottle, with red ribbon, of ginger ale and the ornate biscuit tins and iced cakes, one of which was usually given as a present at Christmas time. Not having much during the year, you appreciated them even more.

Many a child got a sweet and I loved to see Miss Joan, Miss Evelyn and Master Tom (McElderry) coming in to get a sweet like everyone else. My good friend who worked with me in the early days was Katie Wilson. She lived in Townhead Street. In later years Miss Connolly (Annie Mary) worked alongside me as a shop assistant.

By this time there was a larger office staff - all of whom were good friends and many of whom I remember with affection, Miss Trolland and many others.

The years passed quickly. With the 2nd World War came all the business of rationing, with a ration of 2 ozs of butter, 2 ozs tea, 2 ozs sugar and coupons for sweets. I found it hard to keep to this and many a one got a wee bit extra or a little bit of bacon or the like would be saved.

I met many in my days in business, Michael Foot came in with his sister when he was a student, and I saw young children grow up.

I loved working at McElderrys. It was my life. But the money wasn't good - not good at all, there were no yearly pay increases. But I never complained - except once, when I was nearing retirement. I asked for a rise but I never got it. I then left McElderrys, more in sadness than in anger and found myself unemployed for the first time in 37 years. Mr. Beare of Linenhall St., the nearest grocers to McElderrys offered me employment which I took. Mr. McElderry approached Mr. Beare telling him that "Mary should return to my employment" but I didn't . . . and I left Beares.

I was then offered part-time employment by Mr. Clarke, the grocer in Castle St. where Katie was working then. I was well paid. It stamped my cards and there was no need to join the queue at the 'Boru', with only five years to go until I would draw the old age pension. When I came to the age of drawing my old age pension, I faced retirement with regret.

I took over household duties, I had been taught cookery at the Tech. in the early days. By this time we had a range but, although I made good Queen cakes and Christmas cakes and plum jam and crab apple jelly from the orchards of Drumale, my soul still hankered for the hustle and bustle of what was to me a "business world."

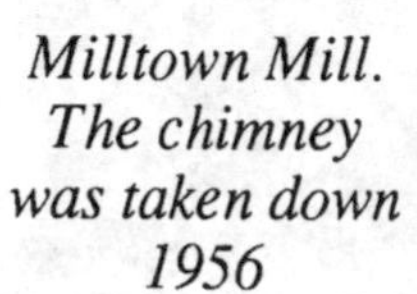

Milltown Mill. The chimney was taken down 1956

Today - Ballymoney Railway Station and The Agivey Bridge, Ballymoney ***Photos: James McGauran***

CHANGE

The first silent films were shown by Barney and Jim O'Kane in the parochial hall using a white sheet and a hand projector. We sat on wooden forms and watched Chaplain and Buster Keaton and marvelled at it all. In the old picture house in Church Street we saw films like Dracula and our first "talkies". The old Y.M.C.A. in Church Street was built in a strange way the floor went up at an angle and down. To keep your balance was difficult in the darkness.

Then came "Bob Kane's Ranch" where we never realised Gene Autry and Hop-a-long Cassidy galloped around the same stone time and time again. Night after night we got value for money. At sixpence for Laurel and Hardy, the Three Stooges, a news reel and the big picture it was more than good value. I listened to Nelson Eddy and Jeanette Mc Donald and watched Shirley Temple. I would have gone to the pictures usually on my half-day, Tuesday, but since there were three changes in the week and I wanted to see Rebecca or Wuthering Heights I'd have stayed over in the town: I finished work at six.

The first time I heard a radio was at the Coronation of George VI and Queen Elizabeth in 1937. Mrs. Kearney at the Milltown invited us to listen with herself and Brigid. Johnny was alive but he must have been busy elsewhere. I had followed the story of Edward and Mrs. Simpson and the Abdication in the papers.

After that we bought a new radio from O'Kanes. It had a little Master's Voice symbol in front like the shape of the old gramophone on which we listened to John Mc Cormack and Caruso and the opera music which John loved so much. "Wet" or acid batteries had to be charged at Warnock's garage on Main Street. They were heavy to carry but we had our favourite programmes, I.T.M.A. and others that we would not have missed. Later my father could listen to Chamberlain and Lord Haw-Haw and all about world affairs, ever ready to engage any visitor who would listen in weighty discussion. Later still we had a radio with a "dry" battery - we bought these in Moffets on Main Street. Now we are in the transistor age. Joe is no teenager but he likes to listen in peace.

When we first got a television and I was about 70 I didn't really feel we would get our value out of it. But we all have. Joe and Andy follow boxing and snooker and football. We all enjoy Mastermind and the Antiques Roadshow and "nature" programmes of all kinds. You might be surprised at many a thing we watch.

Changes just crept up on us. It is not so long since electric light came to the labourers cottages. The old oil lamps were put aside. There was no more trimming of wicks, and polishing

Main Street, Ballymoney.

globes and carrying paraffin from the town. The electric light might not be so kind to old faces and it showed up cobwebs and spiders and daddy-long legs and earwigs, but it was very handy. As a child I was terrified an earwig would get right into my ear. There was no longer any danger of setting the bed on fire and the candle grease dripping as I continued my nightly reading.

Carrying water from the pump is a thing of the past and I'd almost forgotten rubbing shirt collars on the wash-board though I still order Sunlight soap from Pollocks.

Now I am no longer able to walk to the town and Andy can't drive anymore, we get our messages from Pollocks in Castle Street. I still know good tea and cheese (no tea-bags for me) and the look of good bacon. Andy gets angry when I stock-pile tea and sugar and tins of beans and pears and peaches, packets of candles and packets of boxes of matches. I never like to be scarce of anything. I never liked footiness or meaness.

It took me a while to adapt to the "new" money after a lifetime dealing in £. s. d.

The open fire is long gone. We keep a good supply of sticks, logs, turf and coal to stoke our cooker which heats the radiators. Joe is up to light it by 6.30 every morning.

At bedtime the hot water bottles are filled - not an iron wrapped in flannel or an earthenware one any more.

Hiring Fair, Ballymoney around 1922 - 25

W.H. McAfee's around 1904

O'Kane's Wine & Spirit Merchant, Main Street
These premises were originally where the Central Bar is situated nowadays. Patrick Joseph O'Kane (1878-1937) standing outside the business his father, James, started. Patrick also ran a Ford agency, believed to be the first in Ballymoney, and it was situated at the other side of the Billiard Room entrance (also owned by O'Kane's. The Wine and Spirit business ended in 1951

RETRACING MY STEPS

I think I have a photographic memory. I am not so good on days and dates. But Joe could tell you what year old Hugh Hunter was born and what year Willie lost his new cap on a flight over Ballykelly. He could tell you what year Alcock & Brown made the first non-stop transatlantic flight and for how long Joe Louis held the World Heavyweight Boxing Championship.

My memories are nearer home. I wonder if anyone remembers Ned Craft and Blind Jean. There are no beggars going the roads any more in ragged clothes and broken boots.

Black Nancy used to call every Saturday. She got her tea and something to put in her purse, a few vegetables, a bit of bread and more than a grain of tea and sugar before there were any plastic bags. It must have been John christened her the "Rent Collector". I don't know whether is was because she was always asking for something for her rent or just because she came so regularly. If she fancied a few sweet-peas she would have got those too on her way out the gate.

Yankie Kearns lived for a time in a hut on the Bravellan Road. He got odd jobs with farmers. When anyone tried to hurry him he always replied, "Rome wasn't built in a day". There was Orange Paddy who could suit his tune to his audience. When "Kitty, my Love" got tired of "Kitty, my Love, will you marry me. Kitty, my Love, will you go-o. Kitty, my Love, marry me. Either say yes, or say no-o." he checked his wild gig and changed to "There's a happy land".

The oldest Ballymoney inhabitant that I have known - Hugh Hunter 1847 - 1941

Scrubber Tam (McGahey) sold besoms, some times no more than a bundle of twigs tied together. Henry Wallace sold herrings, sixpence a dozen and one extra.

Johnny Woodrow, Willie Mc Kee, Johnny Wales and James Young were in the days of tall horse-drawn vans and unsliced bread.

John Hutchinson, Hugh Lusk and Dummy Mearns were tailors with John in Hamiltons.

You got your shoes half soled with John Shiels at the Railway Bridge. John was a pigeon fancier and so was Cosey Joe Shiels. Paddy McKitterick kept greyhounds. A man got a pair of hob-nailed boots in Stinsons on Main Street. The ladies were fitted by Miss Morrison in the room at the back.

You got your hair cut, both men and women by Lindsey McAuley, before ladies hairdressers became common and permanent waving the order of the day.

If you got a new costume your money zoomed along the little railway from Miss McKeown to the office in H. McCurdy Hamiltons. You could sit on one of the very high chairs at the counter until your change of maybe 3/7 rang back. Mr. Hamilton discussed the weather while you waited.

I've outlived almost everyone in Ballymoney and about it - the McKeevers, Diamonds, Friels, Dillons, McIlvennas, McMullans and Maggie McFall of the Temperence hotel in Main Street. Tom Scott, the nurse McDowells - who taught first aid - and nurse Moran - who helped bring almost every infant in the area into the world for decades after my birth - lived in Charlotte Street.

Further down Charlotte Street in Ishlan lived Miss Peg Pollock who rode her horse down Main Street and out by our house. I knew Miss Pollock well both in the shop and at or Women's Institute meetings. I loved the meetings and our outings.

The Miss Cochranes bought a season ticket to Portrush to treat their little poms to afternoon tea in Portballintrae. Do you remember them pinning a wee broach on your dress on the way to Portrush by train?

Mickey Mallon, the poor man's solicitor, Johnny Trainor, the food controller and Johnny Kearney, Lord Dumping Ground are gone too.

Joe asks me if I mentioned the Logans who lived beside us at Ballybrakes and the Bairds. We still hear from Canada at Christmas.

I can picture them all. I can see Ned O'Neill and even taste his ice cream "sliders" on a hot summer Sunday and smell his chips, peas, and vinegar of a cold Winter's evening as the mill girls climbed down from the lorry from Balnamore singing, "Let him go, let him tarry, let him sink or let him swim . . . . . "

It is all of twenty years since Katie died and touching thirty from the old man died. It is 40 years since I rode out to visit Maggie and Ellen and Jane Mc Donald at Agivey. Mullaghmore was once more grazing for sheep, the airfield being closed, but the many homesteads gone which had housed earlier generations of my mother's people.

It is all of 40 years since wee Mrs. Torrens came in from over the Bann Bridge after her husband died, to live where the Meehans had lived in Castle Street. She was like a little bird. She'd grip my knee telling me some frightful story and send me off into the dark with another Mills and Boon.

It is the best of 50 years since Annie Mc Afee made wartime sandwiches with mashed parsnip and banana essence or read the tea leaves to tell us of the seas we would cross, the money we would get and the great omens of things ahead of us.

It is 50 years since I rode out to Drumale on Sunday 3rd September 1939, to Ellen Dickson's wake on the day war was declared.

It is almost 60 years since my mother died and maybe eighty from I crossed the Bann on the Mail Car.

It is 90 years since I heard the first drums on the Twelfth.

The little robins no longer nest in the gate post for we got a new gate. But the snowdrops and the daffodils come each spring even after the hardest winter.

When first the Institute was formed in 1937
Miss Pollock was made President upon that June 11,
and she is now our Patron Saint nobody will dispute,
With tact, hard work and patience she has made the Institute,
And proves a thing which grows so well has got a healthy root.

And on the first Committee then, among the leading dames,
McCorriston and Cunningham have proudly left their names,
Miss McDowell and Miss Crawford joined up then and join us still,
Like Mrs. Abernethy, Mrs. Herd and Mrs. Hill.
Mrs. Hogg and Keers and Hunter, McQueston, McNamee
McKeever and McKenna and McComb were names to see,
Norris, Thompson, Ross and Patterson and Tomlinson were strong,
If these aren't all Foundationers, they're Members very long.

They held Committees every week, and lovely china got,
Cup, saucer, plate from McAfees cost ninepence for the lot.
They'd people down from Belfast to explain the aims and rules,
Had parties, trips and useful talks, and made some sea-grass stools.
When war broke out in '39 they answered shot for shot,
By preserving garden vegetables, and nearly took a plot.

To do their bit to fight the foe the Institute was willing,
It's well that Hitler didn't know their credit was five shilling!
They gathered hips, sold tickets and clothed evacuees,
And knitted socks and scarves and gloves for sailors on the seas.
Miss Pollock soon decided with the help of Mr. Lawlor,
(The navy being over-socked) they must adopt a trawler!

And looking back on those old days, though numbers now are stronger,
We think of Members with us then, who are with us now no longer.
We have a card of Membership which tells our aims and ends,
And we try to make it more than just a cracky crowd of friends.
But we can't beat other Institutes, no matter how we try
With part songs out of Handel, and Boat Songs out of Skye!
Headquarters cups have missed us, but, Miss Pollock, do not fret,
We'll weave and stitch at objects which will win your Trophy yet.
Some of us were successful between the two Novembers,
Mrs. Bannon, Mrs. Torrens have produced two future members!

Wee boys may tramp about above, and draughts sweep round the floor,
But our hearts are warm with those we love, and who can ask for more?

The End of the Road

Harry Lauder used to sing about it and Jamie Stewart was Ballymoney's Harry Lauder on the stage of old. When I said I didn't feel any older than nine or nineteen it is true, but only half true. The last years have been good years but those in McElderrys were the happiest. If I told you I say a prayer for R.A. every night with those for all the rest would you think it odd.

Enlighten me oh Lord, I've lost the lease of things. It's odd, for I was never tongue tacked. I'm not ready yet to meet my Maker but I am coming to the rear of things. You know where the good sheets, pillow-cases, white quilts are and the blessed candles. But there might be another chapter in me yet - maybe even two.

"The American Clock which was given along with the Bible by my Grandmother Crawford to each of her married sons"

Events Which Touched Mary in her Lifetime

1901	Death of Queen Victoria.
1909	Old age pension introduced for the first time.
1912	Sinking of the Titanic.
1914	Home Rule Bill passed by the House of Commons. The Great War began.
1922	Irish Free State established.
1926	Pensions for widows and orphans. General strike in Great Britain.
1927	Wireless telephone service to New York inaugurated. Lindbergh flew the Atlantic alone.
1936	Outbreak of Spanish Civil War.
1937	Coronation of King George VI and Queen Elizabeth.
1939	Germany invaded Poland. Britain declares war on Germany.
1940	Food rationing begins.
1945	Germany surrenders. 1946 National Health Service Act introduced.
1953	Princess Victoria foundered.
1954	Food rationing ends.
1958	U.S. launches first moon rocket.
1961	Yuri Gargarin first man in space.
1969	U.S. astronaut Neil A. Armstrong first man to step on moon. British troops ordered to N. Ireland.
1972	Bloody Sunday. Stormont Parliament suspended.
1975	Margaret Thatcher takes over as leader of the Conservative Party.

In loving memory of

Mary Crawford

who died in Robinson Hospital Ballymoney
15 February 1990
Aged 94

Andrew Crawford

who died in Coleraine Hospital
27 June 1990
Aged 85

Joseph Crawford

who died in Royal Victoria Hospital Belfast
11 July 1990
Aged 82

and all the rest